EARTH SCIENCE

PUBLISHED BY 421 ATLANTA IN 2016

421 Second Avenue NE
Atlanta, GA 30317
www.421atlanta.com

ISBN 13: 978-0-9906020-3-3

Book design by Adam Robinson and Amy McDaniel.
Cover image: "The Heavens" by Reuben Potter, *Voice From the Heavens, or Stellar & Celestial Worlds* (1890)

EARTH SCIENCE

SARAH GREEN

Sam

For Neil, whose writing I'm looking forward to getting to know. Happy Spring! Sarah

421 atlanta

Atlanta, GA

4/18

P O E M S

I.

II.

III.

FOR PETER CAMPION

I.

JULY LINDEN

At first I thought it was a grape arbor
or a guest's jasmine shampoo.
I would walk around barefoot
after a glass of wine
on the sidewalk, holding up a leaf
and sniffing—not this, not that,
it was not my house, I was only feeding
a couple's fish and sleeping lightly
on the woman's side. The man's end table
held spectacles and vitamins, hers
a goofy stuffed monster, Portuguese books
on tape, and I never fully closed
the blinds at night, the better to see
old starry neighborhoods I missed.
The better to eavesdrop
on a swaying couple in the parking lot—
shadowy heart to heart,
I will never ... sweatshirt to sweatshirt,
Don't say that ... one friend leaning against a car

reading his phone. *You have to get your life together…*
Neighbors yelling *It's 3 am!*

That city tree coming in
like a tide, like a piece of music
or embroidery, then sailing off, I still didn't know
it was a tree. It started to unlock me,
I started to leave the porch door open while
I slept through firecrackers almost but not quite
blowing off teens' hands, and someone could have
climbed the balcony and stabbed me
for whatever reason
people stab women sometimes,
but they had better things to do,
like watch TV. Feeling a need
to check the door, halfway through the night,
I finally didn't trip over my shoes in the hall
because I could see, the moon was full,
and the fish that had been sick got better
and started eating more, even built the foam nest
male bettas make when they're happy.
So I bragged about that, feeling responsible.

And the owner replied, from Brazil, *Cute,*
but it's sad, too, isn't it. He thinks he lives in an ocean.
He thinks he's changing his life.

BON BON

That donkey—
there's so much I don't know about my life.

I've called him a "baby" in stories,
but was he full grown and just miniature?

I've said he chased my writer friend and me
along a gravel road in Burgundy. It's true.

We passed the driveway where he grazed,
or begged, or head-butted his colleagues,

or waited for his owner to come home, whatever,
my friend sought advice on his one-act

about Israel and Palestine.
Maybe the audience would sit on stage.

The donkey charged at us—
it sounds silly—as if to gore us like a bull

then let us be, then sprinted toward our backs,
stopping again when we both turned around

and then he ran back to his yard.
This happened several times.

"Oh that's Bon Bon" our host laughed later,
and we laughed. He was a serious donkey

doing his job, guarding the house.
He was a young donkey, playing.

It was a strange town, come to think of it.
Certain mornings, the white Charolois cows,

kneeling, would low
call-and-response style, across three hills.

And then they'd all rise to their feet.

ASSEMBLY

While the bombers were playing basketball
or smoking weed and powering up a level on Xbox, I was falling a
    little out of my tube top

down the street from them at Christina's Ice Cream, dropping my
    sunglasses, trying free
spoonfuls: rose, cucumber, chocolate, green tea.

Last summer, I still hoped a certain man might change his mind.
I swam. I watched The Bachelorette. The loudest noise was my
    neighbor once a week

at the fire hydrant setting a blue bin full of rinsed-out bottles down.
    Next door, all three
triple-decker porches glowed at 6 PM from solar lanterns. The
    bombers were not bombers

yet, just brothers, both younger than me, wrestling. I had some
    things on my mind,

like which sandwich to buy—while I waited, a very old waitress put
    up her feet.

She was wearing compression stockings. Last summer, the younger
    brother decided to grow
out his hair because girls liked it. The right lung of one of my
    friends showed a dark spot,

another friend called me in tears about a pregnancy she didn't want,
    I cried
when a third friend called, finally pregnant. I was happy for her. I
    traipsed in flip-flops

for some peach muffins, some iced coffee. Men asked did I need
    help carrying groceries?
Men argued, loud, outside the mechanic's, about Red Sox trades.
    We were all very alive—

all of us and the brothers. *Who cares?* the bombers began to say, I
    guess, and then believe.

MY LEASE

Every day, the hammering next door

   shakes my threshold.

   In Nepal, x finger-widths from me,

my friend Jen in the new earthquake

says *there's a man telling us all to hug.*

She takes a picture of him. *My new friend Ramesh.*

   Tell my kids I'm fine.

Also, I'm never doing this again.

   I love her for the last sentence.

We want to be a helper "on the ground."

   Except when the ground moves.

There was a dogwood I'd visit because it changed

    like it was going first

to help me learn. At night outside the student center

    I'd watch it flare and fade

but stay. *The car has persisted through a change,*

    my sophomore year Metaphysics textbook said,

we'd all agree,

though I have given it a coat of paint,

it's the same car. The next question was

    how many changes can it undergo

and still be that car? My friend said of the pillar

    at the Camino de Santiago

it was not enough to look at it. He needed to kiss it.

    But it was behind bars

to bolster it

from too many pilgrims who'd worn it down.

It would still be the pillar even if pilgrim kisses

    caused it to crumble into dust,

that's what he thought. But it would not still be holy

    if no one made it holy

with their touch. I want to put a velvet rope around

    my dawn and then have it be dawn

for a long time, alone with my coffee. While trees rustle

    and birds keep the borders alive,

the sky a pale sheet on a clothesline in the wind.

    Let change come in a way I can picture.

Now that I've gotten used to

grumbling at the hammers,

they fall silent. Now that it's silent,

    my lease is up.

SEEING HIS NEW GIRLFRIEND AT THE COAT CHECK

The only thing to do was turn
my back and slowly be the opposite
of a stripper, it was winter, I'd checked

a hoodie and a vest and a parka I eased
into, I prepped the antidote: reverse
of every curve he bought for free,

I gathered fleece, static, metal, and down,
stretching my arms, not snow angel,
or spread-eagled in his old bed,

I had the floor, I was the negative,
he'd loved me, too, this was the speed
at which, to make him beg, I moved—

WATCHING
THE CRANES

Watching the cranes
pour into Platte River
like floating black letters,
a note dictated

to pink evening sky I miss
my grandfather's scrub pines
and the clothesline suspended
there and I miss the old space

between chipped piano keys,
the way a stuck key lets you imagine
all sounds in its place, so you can say
you'd hammer righteously

that humid key
if it were playable, but instead
you are stuck with silence
and ecology is stuck with you,

naked human on hot summer night,
one of us taking a turn
being the river, one of us taking
a turn being the bird.

OUR BIRD

Red as the nine of hearts,
Our bird perused local grasses.

"Ours", like "our song", by love's
Colonial logic. *House Finch.*

I thought he'd have a cooler name—

A name to get across the rarity—
But nothing's rarer than a home.

"I gave my love a rare ring," Anon brags.
A verse later—older, wiser—

She gives that same love a chicken.

SNOW DELAY

She thought I was studying *poultry*,
that woman in line at the airport, a veterinarian

herself. Outside, Chicago emptied out its white
sugar. In a few minutes I'd be panicking

on the plane, while a young Dominican guy
ate a tuna fish sandwich, pausing once in awhile

to wipe his mouth. He and I'd both fall asleep
deep as children, then wake up close.

His mom in Queens not doing so well.
Eight weeks in this new city. He's still lonely.

It's poetry, I said, clutching my puffy coat.
Cheap down feathers sticking to my shirt.

TOWELS

Why were there never enough towels
in the guesthouse run by Benedictine nuns in Italy?
Because the nuns wanted to save water.

Why did the nuns want to save water?
Because they were poor and also wanted to save soap
and electricity consumed by tourists blow-drying their hair

and spilling self-tanner on the bedspread.
Why were we blow-drying our hair? To look hot.
Why were they poor? Because they took a vow of poverty.

Why did they take a vow of poverty? Why are people poor?
Why did Jesus say, "The poor you will always have with you"?
They took a vow to live in solidarity with poor people

who there will always be as long as you and I
take vows of wealth. What's wealth? It's like a wish
to always have enough towels, not just enough, hundreds

more towels than we need. How many towels do we need?
Enough to soak up all the water on the blue tiles
from the glass shower with the bent door, so it doesn't drip

down to the nuns' quarters where they have lived so long
not touching men, or being touched by men, or being seen
by anyone except tourists, to whom they feed fresh bread

and strong coffee, for whom they mop the floor, and pray,
tourists who track in little microbes from the street,
little scraps of song. Little sunlit gap the grocer passes

baskets through in the morning, then a receipt. Then he rings
his bicycle's thin bell and pedals quickly back into his life,
so separate from the life of nuns, he thinks, *poor nuns. Poor*

us, I think, *thinking God's something to go find or to deny.*

BRUNO MARS

My student Amy says Bruno Mars the singer seems sincere
about wanting his ex to be happy. He loves her so much,
he hopes her new man buys her flowers.
Crystal, ten years older than Amy, offers: He feels regret.
Patrick says he's talking to himself, telling himself
not to fuck up next time. To buy the next woman flowers.
Delia says Not all women want flowers. Haley agrees,
causing a ricochet in that chair row
of quick high fives.
Evan says He's trying to win her back. He hasn't learned
anything. It's a ruse. He doesn't want her to be happy.
He wants her to be happy with him. Delia says God,
to hear this song five times a day on the radio—
Haley says We do. Delia says I mean as the girlfriend.
She'll never come back, Crystal says.
He's learning, Patrick says.
Amy says, again, he seems sincere.

FATE FACTORY

Did the three fates choose their own fates?

Why would anyone want to spin, measure and cut

eternally? Why are there three? For bathroom breaks?

Is there a window

looking out over the city from Fate Factory

like the one on Beacon Street

outside my old office window? Do the fates,

like me, practice stretching their eyesight right there

like some magazine told them they should, or some radio doctor,

I guess they don't have time to read, noting distant jet streams,

white type on water towers, a dozen school children holding a rope,

wing-like flickers between buildings? Are the fates paid?

Is virtue seriously its own reward? Is my head so over-full

of aphorisms from the past, the future's aphorisms stand no chance?

Will I always be here, bumper to bumper on manifesto bridge

and have to pee? Is that what Dustin meant

in 2011, sliding his coaster at the bar

closer to me? When he said, *Can you prove I'm here*

right now of my free will? Can you prove I'm not?

FINDINGS

for my brother

Today a deaf man shouted *Hey*—
Hey—as I moved to trade the warm bus

for snowfall. I stopped. He was holding
a pale green hat

which had slipped my gloved hands
in the rush from seat to door.

I turned, wondering, saw
the hat, his headphones, light eyes,

said *Thanks*, then, *Thanks*, again, clutching
the wool. Other bus riders looking

back, looking around. Later,
stir-frying for one, turmeric yellowing

my fingers like pollen, I remember
some Hindus believe there's this

great heat we start to give off
in our saddest times. A sort

of stubborn fever—rising, signaling, until
even the gods

feel their warm foreheads, put down their
magazines, call out our names.

INSECT

Listening to my neighbor's
record—all techno traffic
beats and outer space—it's
like borrowing someone
else's thick skin. Like

when I wore your Red
Sox coat and followed you
into porch smoke, because
I thought I saw a light on
in our loneliness.

SKELETON EVENINGS

Just a few layers between my skeleton and this lottery ticket, these shopping bags, these pears, this snow, these strangers shoveling. I do not slip. I cross when the cars stop. I watch the light go

pink and sentimental between bus routes, lost gloves, change, I grind my teeth. My skeleton is unknown now to archaeologists but has a weight and age they could test for, I am not

Egyptian or a bog girl from long ago, I was not buried with jewelry, or with someone, I carry home discount roses, I take the stairs, I curse the dark landing, I turn the key.

II.

SHRIMP BOATS

When my grandmother sang about shrimp boats,
I thought she was singing about how they were far away,
how we wished we were up close and could see them.
I didn't know that she was singing about time.
It took North Carolina–percent humidity,
vague green tendrils, back road gravel
white as white noise, three lamps glowing
in strangers' living rooms, the sun still up at 8 pm,
chalk streaks of clouds, brooding magnolias,
a tarp over the pool behind a stranger's fence
thirty years later for me to understand.
How familiar this evening has always been,
under my life, close as the horse behind the fence.
How soft the air against my face
in that spare bed, facing the beach at night,
my grandmother singing
while hanging bathing suits to dry, lights blinking
far away on decks of the same boats
inside her song, lights I could see, the ocean dark,

the gulls hidden. I thought the minor key was there
in honor of the dead turtle we saw that day, my first
dead thing, dead on its back, soapy with loam.
The ocean washing over it—
me with my little pail. I was the *baby safe at home,*
the waves *crashing in,* somewhere men *toiling,*
or that's what the song said, the boats much farther
than the last sandbar, where I was not allowed,
where I would someday go.

CONSTELLATIONS

Across the room at the party
after we weren't speaking any more:
a thread of small lights
between my shoulder and his shoulder.
Both shoulders kind-of-turned.
Lights that were, to be honest,
just wine glasses refracting
intermittent blinking from a Christmas tree.
Glasses in hands of bystanders
who were not bystanders in their own account
of the evening, taking part, gracious, in real,
non-subtext-filled conversations.
Bare calves and knees of mini-skirted girls
on couches, men standing up straight
when asked about the kids, the kids are good,
the dog had to be put down,
he was a good dog, yes, the wife's almost done
with her MD. I tried to look somehow
without looking, my back to him.

My heart lurched as far as it could
to his side of my chest but it could not fly
physically through it. Once
at the grocery store, I sensed him behind me,
two aisles away, and I knew we were missing
each other. Glad to reconvene at the counter.
His greeting arm. A little kiss while the receipt
Printed. This was not that. Whenever
one of us arrives somewhere to rest, the other rises,
swift, from that place, mathematically.
Constellations, I think—one law
keeps us from moving closer. Another says
we have to share a hemisphere.
We're not famous, though.
We don't have real names.
Try to see us, we're hidden by clouds.

SUNDAY AFTERNOON, SPAIN

I wanted to stay lost in the cool synagogue,
Spanish with frescoes
arching over me gold and blue lazuli,
outside high noon and getting hotter,
our bus farther and farther away, somewhere
our bodies were mapped to be before we strayed.

WONG KAR WAI'S
"FALLEN ANGELS"

Is it still dripping?
The colander of June cherries
you brought into the dark
living room and the small empty bowl
for cherry stones

Saturday noon, the blinds closed
against sharp Harvard light
yesterday's office shirt rumpled,
you tapping your cigarette hand
too far away while the VCR whirred

On the coffee table,
a sympathy card two years old
for your dead father (why was it still there?)
Your roommates sleeping, every dish dirty,
the kitchen trash blocking the door

How lodged, askew, that summer
spit of cherry stones,
your sadness smudged on all the furniture,
my sadness played by the Chinese girl,
your hand bored by my knee

ROOM TEMPERATURE

One of those mornings before the fight
that meant we'd never acknowledge each other
again, could never take
anything back, I thought, If I marry him,

it will still be like this: same grapefruit soap
from Trader Joe's, mildewed shower lining,
same sweet grass smell at the back of his neck,
wine on his breath. On the dresser:

same wallet, pills, phone, lighter, keys. If
I were his wife, at breakfast we'd still rarely
meet each other's gaze, he'd crawl into my arms
after some failure and it would become

my failure too, to pay the rent, to feel like a hero.
I'd still wonder who he dreamed of.
Only in bed, still, would anyone smile. Even then
it would mean pretending

there was no ongoing world, and I wasn't
restless, bright blank noons he muttered "Stay,"
then fell asleep, the curtains drawn, heavy.
Did I want that?

A.C. spinning
its same white noise, its preset cool,
canceling out my faint girl heat,
motoring down to 68, then dropping off,

seeming almost alert to his small snore,
like it knew him best. It was here before me.
It would be here, too, after. It had seen when,
how, why I'd fallen, it knew already

where I'd fall—soon, forever, in the lineup
of almost-wives. The shirt I'd recently borrowed
was one my jilted predecessor left.
But I didn't know. I lay watching

his giant and dim sleep, cluster of freckles
below his eye, at his cheekbone. His jeans
over a chair, the belt still in them. His soft earlobe.
I wanted all that. I didn't need trees,

or a good book on the train, or anyone
to warn me.

HOTEL WINTER

The dark is a way of moving.
The wait is a place.
Zero filled me with its virile

nothings. Sweet, I know—zero—
the dark's a weight. The weight's
a place to let your truck run

off the road, uphill
where other wheels have gone
before you. The move's the way

station. The stay's one night,
the dark's sable, the dark's a stall
for a stallion named zero

with a moving mane.
There is no wait in vain.

AFTER A
DISAPPOINTMENT

The taxi driver's name is Tino.
For some reason, the way he throws
his kind voice toward me—telling me

how the famous Constantine walked
his mother, Helen, uphill with him
to dig the Holy Cross out of the dirt—

it makes the streetlights blurry, astigmatic.
Until I blink again, and here's a stop sign,
a pizza place, the meter ticking.

Just before this, during the famous author's
reading, I thought about hummingbirds.
Does that sugar water ever work? Up front,

a shy blond man kept turning to catch his
girlfriend's eye and blushing. Minutes later,
doing it again. This summer, my mother

found a hummingbird feeder, still boxed,
dusty from a basement shelf, and sent it
forward to my dad's new house.

HIGH SCHOOL

Jane's car orbited
my home like a science lesson
about Saturn's rings.

But I was slowed down
from leaving. Jane's Mustang's red,
used to be aqua—

I said to the floor,
pink azalea May,
I don't know why I'm living.

Jane said we're here
to figure it out. She said *Dead*
you're just in space

floating around. I floated
around the phone. She said
I'm coming to get you.

Galaxies affixed themselves
to the family roof.
My dad said *Don't*

you dare go down those stairs.
His voice climbed, fell, landed
with the fertilizer and the potting soil.

Forever I stayed up thinking about
hanging up the phone, listening
to scrapes of skateboards on sidewalks,

watching for headlights,
waiting so long that summer came.

BLUE HOUR

It's all—yesterday—it's sweet behind me
like a low branching sun you'd turn your head for,

like a red-haired woman, like somebody's one
good song. I could do worse, humming.

I'm telling you, all the shades—my father's glass
of wine, my brother's Red Sox hat, my mother's

shirt, that glow of white—they worked their way
into a new kind of color. We tucked our hair behind

our ears. We drank our ice. We were gorgeous
in the eyes of our soup spoons.

AFTERWORD

But I can't remember
if your father burned the field—
what was it now, for the ice skaters? He set it on fire?
Teenagers giggling,
heads bent, arms around each other's waists,
white skates tossed over their shoulders, their plaid coats,
the blades dangling. You were remembering the smoke.
Or was it the neighbor's yard? The neighbor's fire?
What season? I said.
Late fall, you answered, and the burnt leaves
blew around us in your half-raised hospital bed.

ACTUALLY NO ONE WAS TAP DANCING

Actually no one was sweating
in some third story with waxed floors.
Actually no scratchy record was playing
Tchaikovsky to ungrateful schoolgirls
stretching their arabesques higher
higher, striving for the smooth line
from ponytail to pointed toe. Actually
no ten-year-old, tan, fresh out of
gymnastics camp, was congratulated
on her summer-flat belly in a room
teary with mirrors. If it sounded like
clumsy metal on wood, the out-of-step
scuff of shiny patent leather, stopping
and starting again, it wasn't. As a matter
of fact, it was a teenage boy running
a stick along a black railing. *Flap-shuffle,*
shuffle, ball-change. Slight frown. Fierce as
his thoughts, the real live sun, setting.

THE PRESENT

It was like this. Golden light was on the tip of my tongue. Every building had a cat's eye, a handful of jacks, Bazooka gum, one good dress, and a rotary phone. My dad looked up from his legal pad and became a boy in Michigan again behind his glasses. I checked the card catalog for "tornado" just in case. Somebody's grocery cart went skidding out and hit the tracks. Somebody's hat got wedged, somebody's quarter fell between seat cushions. On weekends my allowance increased microscopically. Everyone chopped onions and sizzled hamburger. Somebody stuck a record jacket in my hands.

III.

BEFORE

What did I do with the encyclopedia set
from A for afternoon to Zenith of morning
back when I'd foolishly loaned out the L volume
between Breakfast and Work,
forgot which party was responsible,
there was no order form, it had been a gift
that neatly fit two antique shelves, it was rare
to find one book for sale alone, without starting over
as if learning the alphabet again, which I could not afford.
I knew the alphabet, I liked Coffee, I studied Trees,
I cooked Moroccan food. I must have watched
the same commercial twenty times so as not to notice
how the books leaned on each other but could not hide
the hour before bed it would have filled to pore through L:
lemur, Louisiana Purchase, love, lodestar. The latitude
and longitude of that hour.

THERE'S BEEN A MISCOMMUNICATION ABOUT MY PAST SNAKE SKINS

I didn't intend them for the town archive.
They don't apply, now, to *this* me.
I intended to slip away and down a riverbank
and through a log, or a tire. Some reeds—
I left so many skins.
Don't gather them. Don't come looking.
I'm in a field, feeling ready to be a different snake.
Snake 17.
Thank you, but buy a snake skin purse,
a pair of snake skin shoes. Wear them yourself.
Think about how it would feel to be a snake.
It would feel like witness protection.
It would feel like exiting
without having entered a door. When I lie down,
I call that "waiting for my next mission."
And then I shake that mission off of me.

OMENS

She said: I don't look for omens
Because none come to me.
Because I can't find them—
Here come the starlings
In their non-pattern, the church bells
Fighting over two worn tunes.
I don't drink tea. I read my horoscope
The way my colorblind husband
Once chose his ties. I love the stutter
Of a motorcycle at a light,
Unmusical,
The paper thrown at my doorstep
That wakes me up.
I get up then.
My knees ache when it snows—
That's air pressure. I throw apples
to the raccoons.

THE MARINES'
EX-PRIEST, ACROSS
FROM ME AT THE
LENTEN FISH FRY

"I was new. What took
getting used to was,
they'd ask my permission.

Permission to use first person?
I'd say, *Granted.*
They'd say, *I need your help.*

You see,
they're not supposed to go by 'I'.
Always *This recruit. This recruit seeks*

such-and-such. South Carolina—
Many did prison time
before they came, or drugs.

They stop that pretty quick.
Funny,
there's someone shouting

in their face all day *You're nothing*,
but it makes them feel, you know,
they are something,

surviving it. That there's some place
inside of them.

Inside us—look, no matter what
we lose, we have to make the loss
into a place. A holy place.

The eulogy I gave today?
A mother's healthy three month old.

A mystery. What could I say?
Time won't heal that."
He stops to add more tartar

to his fried fish plate.
He bows his head.

SALT PEANUTS

My dad in the neonatal ICU as a med student
was kind of responsible, at least for five minutes,
for keeping all of those babies alive,
but he tried not to think about it.
He adjusted miniature IVs.
He recorded vital signs on charts and signed as
illegibly as possible, to seem official.
The babies didn't know how frail they were.
They thought they were normal puppies.
They thought he was their dog mother.
But the machines were how they ate and breathed.
The machines in charge of keeping track
of heart function sounded like dripping tap water,
or, at times, the silver resonance of a tuning fork.
The sounds crossed.
There was almost a steady rhythm.
There was almost a tune—
"Salt Peanuts" by Dizzy Gillespie, my dad thought,
but none of the nurses had heard of it.

They heard heart monitors. They had clean sheets to fold.
So he had to wait thirty years to tell me and my brother,
in the car on the way to dinner, as if he heard
our healthy hearts and lungs pumping, and thought of it,
as if we were old enough now.

WHEN IT HAPPENS

Of course the trees are pressing in like visitors

at a crèche scene although it's June, and that means

they're the newcomers. Squeaky green leaves—

Of course blue sky: *don't look at me,*

I'm no umpire. If someone could bring in a psychic please,

shouldn't be hard, this is New York City. Not really, no—

The question is how long should the organ donation people

wait to knock. There is a protocol,

a level of activity after which that activity

will never change. They say. For those not in the room,

there is a sense the color will drain out

of the evening, although it's still so light. When it happens,

that's how they'll know. If he is dead, he must be able to travel

outside his bathed and clothed body, here to this park:

bikers flickering in and out of view, how do members of that one tribe

in New Guinea describe someone even just temporarily

out of their sight: *he has now passed from existence*

although he's just around a hill.

I CAN'T STOP IT

That jonquil spray:

    notes from a bird

lilac and soil

    I can't stop it from reaching me

Invisible staff   clef

thrusting its pistil melody

    due to some genes

It can't stop it either

    Why aren't we all

a little more anxious

    re: beauty

re: Helen launching our ship

    continually

whether our ship's ready or not

    It must be exhausting

to be so beautiful

    my friend said to his ex

as if even naked

    her raiment was so heavy

Maybe he meant the exhaustion

    of slinging casual arrows

into the hearts of onlookers

    watching them fall

although the bird has no idea

it arrests me

OCTOBER RECOVERY

Coming down from the train
of sickness, stepping onto the platform

in this thin city, clear air.
No one to greet me. Cold blue sky.

Waking, as if into
a pressed shirt. That scent,

steamwater and sweat.
Folded papers in my hand.

I'm in my own bed. Landmarks: a steeple,
cut off by my windowsill.

The neighbor's dog typing away
on the wood floor.

Cracker crumbs in my sheets.
Michael, I thought of you piling cairns

of white stones, between sadnesses,
your body by now a kind of pillar,

a station. In fever dreams, I could feel
the candles you're lighting

for them in South Boston. I wanted to tell you,
the dead will find the fruit you leave.

PASTELS

I don't know *this* morning, with its glissandos
at rest in sheet music of small children,
still-unfamiliar chateaux tucked in the blind spots
of its fat hillsides. Spring seems
predictable as an anthem. Trees, flowers, bees,
timed fireworks; dawn's parade float
of quilted clouds. One barely has to look at it.
Why can I barely look at it.

EARTH SCIENCE

Why does everyone have to say "It's not real pizza"?
What's realer than my dad, quiet at the Greek restaurant

with the Acropolis half hidden by a plant,
in Bedford, Mass., ordering us both slices, him late from work

during the trial separation, so late that it was dark enough,
waiting at school, to do my science homework: *Find, then draw,*

Cassiopeia. Mornings, the worksheet said *next draw the sun*
over the neighbor's house, for several days, *watch it move left*

as autumn progresses. I would have thought that it stood still.

ACKNOWLEDGMENTS

Gettysburg Review. "After a Disappointment."
North Dakota Quarterly. "Hotel Winter."
Medical Journal of Australia. "Salt Peanuts."
Passages North. "October Recovery."
Pleiades. "Shrimp Boats."
Sixth Finch. "Watching The Cranes" and "Assembly."
The Congeries. "Bruno Mars."

Many thanks to Finishing Line Press for publishing my 2015 chapbook, *Skeleton Evenings*, in which versions of several of these poems appear.

Thanks, too, to the Oberlin College Letterpress Project under the direction of Ed Vermue, which published "The Present" as part of my first chapbook *Temporary Housing*.

A huge thanks to Chad Reynolds for "secret-scouting" this book, and to Amy McDaniel of 421 Atlanta for believing in it. Thank you to Mark Halliday, Jill Rosser, Morgan Frank,

Gabrielle Calvocoressi, Jill McDonough, Daniel B. Johnson, David Young, Martha Collins, Adrienne Su, Katie Berta, Claire Eder, David Rivard, Patrick Swaney, Dustin Faulstick, and Stacy Peters, for their generous and bright assistance with this manuscript. Thanks as well to the Vermont Studio Center for the snowy, pensive, January residency with which it gifted me. And, finally, to the Somerville and Cambridge, MA, singer/songwriter community for teaching me to be brave.

Sarah Green is the author of *Skeleton Evenings*, which won the 2014 New Women's Voices Prize. She lives and teaches in Minneapolis, Minnesota.